PUBLICOLA

OBSERVATIONS ON PAINE'S RIGHTS OF MAN
IN A SERIES OF LETTERS

John Quincy Adams

Liberty's Lamp Books
QUINCY, MA

Copyright © 2014 by Liberty's Lamp Books.

Printed in the United States of America

All rights reserved. No part of this publication may be reproduced, distributed or transmitted in any form or by any means, including photocopying, recording, or other electronic or mechanical methods, without the prior written permission of the publisher, except in the case of brief quotations embodied in critical reviews and certain other noncommercial uses permitted by copyright law. For permission requests, write to the publisher, addressed "Attention: Permissions Coordinator," at the address below.

Cover design by LLPix Designs
www.LLPix.com

Cover paintings: John Adams by John Singleton Copley, 1783; John Quincy Adams by John Singleton Copley, 1796; Thomas Jefferson by Charles Wilson Peale, 1791; Edmund Burke by James Barry, 1771; Thomas Paine by Auguste Millière, 1880, after an engraving by William Sharp, after George Romney, 1792.

Liberty's Lamp Books
377 Willard Street #338
Quincy, MA 02169
www.LibertysLampBooks.com

Book Layout ©2013 BookDesignTemplates.com

Library of Congress Cataloging-in-Publication Data

ISBN 978-0-9911175-2-9

Publicola. Observations on Paine's Rights of man / by John Quincy Adams

Contents

Introduction by Will Butts

Letter I.

Letter II.

Letter III.

Letter IV.

Letter V.

Letter VI.

Letter VII.

Letter VIII.

Letter IX.

Letter X.

Letter XI.

INTRODUCTION

In the late eighteenth century, it was not uncommon for public matters to be discussed and debated in the many newspapers of the time, or through the printing of lengthy pamphlets. And frequently in these publications, opinions were expressed anonymously, or under a pseudonym. Such was the case with *Publicola,* a series of essays by John Quincy Adams, written in the form of letters to Benjamin Russell, editor of the *Columbian Centinal.*

The letters of *Publicola* were written as a refutation of Thomas Paine's *The Rights of Man,* and also in reaction to a controversy that had erupted between the author's father, John Adams, and Thomas Jefferson – a controversy relating to a "pamphlet war" between Thomas Paine and Edmund Burke – and all in the context of the French Revolution.

In 1789, the people of France revolted against their government. In defiance of their king and aristocracy, they first formed their own assembly. Then, upon threat from the king's soldiers, they stormed the Bastille in Paris, freed its dissident prisoners, seized its store of gunpowder, and subsequently killed and beheaded both the governor of the Bastille, and the mayor of Paris. The people of France then proceeded to dismantle their government piece by piece, vesting ever increasing power in a single National Assembly.

In America, one particular pair of eyes followed the events in France with deep concern and foreboding. John Adams, Vice-President of the United States, had read deeply about government. Indeed, Benjamin Rush had claimed that Adams possessed "more learning probably, both ancient and modern, than any man who subscribed the Declaration of Independence."[1]

Adams was also thoroughly familiar with revolutions, having been an active participant in the American Revolution from its very beginning. Furthermore, with his *Thoughts on Government,* Adams had counseled the American colonies on how best to structure their governments once they secured their independence from Britain, for Adams knew, as he wrote later, "it is of great importance to begin well; misarrangements now made will have great, extensive and distant consequences."[2]

Thus, being so well-versed in both history and government, and having also lived in France for several years as negotiator for peace with Great Britain, John Adams was in a unique position to foresee the likely consequences of France's current, perilous path. So with Congress out of session and with time on his hands, Adams began to write.

In April of 1790, Adams began to publish, anonymously, a series of essays entitled *Discourses on Davila,* essentially a translation of Enrico Caterino Davila's *Historia delle guerre civili di Francia* (History of the civil wars of France). Interspersed with Adams' own insights on government in relation to the recent actions of the French, the *Davila* essays were intended to both remind the French people of their history and to caution them of the dangers and pitfalls of single-assembly legislatures and unbalanced governments:

> The men of letters in France are wisely reforming one feudal system; but may they not, unwisely, lay the foundation of another? A legislature, in one assembly, can have no other termination than in civil dissension, feudal anarchy, or simple monarchy.[3]

> If the common people are advised to aim at collecting the whole sovereignty in single national assemblies ... or at the abolition of the regal executive authority; or at a division of the executive power ... they will fail of their own desired liberty, as certainly as emulation and rivalry are founded in human nature, and inseparable from civil affairs. It is not to flatter the passions of the people, to be sure, nor is it the way to obtain a present enthusiastic popularity, to tell them that in a single assembly they will act as arbitrarily and tyrannically as any despot, but it is a sacred truth, and as demonstrable as any proposition whatever, that a sovereignty in a single assembly must necessarily, and will certainly be exercised by a majority, as tyrannically as any sovereignty was every exercised by kings or nobles. And if a balance of passions and interests is not scientifically concerted, the present struggle in Europe will be little beneficial to mankind, and produce nothing but another thousand years of feudal fanaticism, under new and strange names.[4]

The nation which will not adopt an equilibrium of power must adopt a despotism. There is no other alternative. Rivalries must be controlled, or they will throw all things into confusion; and there is nothing but despotism or a balance of power which can control them.[5]

Governments with all power vested in a single assembly were historically prone to rapid dissolution into anarchy. Through his *Davila* essays, Adams was attempting to warn the French, to prevent what would, in his learned view, result in blood and tyranny, leading inevitably to dictatorship, and then to war.

But instead of being received as a warning, Adams' *Davila* essays caused a public firestorm. The French were thought to be following the Americans' lead, by ridding themselves of their monarchy and aristocracy, and setting up a republican government of their own; a government of, by, and for the people. The idea that such a prominent player in the American Revolution would openly decry a similar revolution in France was alarming.

Adams was dealing with reality, to be sure, with the nature of man and of governments, using the examples of the past to foretell the future, but to his detriment, he came across as being in favor of monarchy and aristocracy. He was accused of spending too much time in Europe, of being corrupted by their ways, and of abandoning the republican principles he had once championed.

But John Adams was not the only prominent figure denouncing the events in France. In Britain, Dr. Richard

Price, preacher and philosopher, had given a sermon entitled *A Discourse on the Love of our Country*, which applauded the revolution in France, comparing it with the Glorious Revolution of England in 1688. In reaction to this sermon, Edmund Burke, the British statesman who had so enthusiastically supported the American Revolution, now took to the floor of the British Parliament, to refute Dr. Price and to excoriate the French for their actions:

> The French have proved themselves the ablest architects of ruin that ever existed in the world. In one summer they have done their business ... in this very short space of time they have completely pulled down to the ground their monarchy, their church, their nobility, their law, their revenue, their army, their navy, their commerce, their arts, and their manufacturers ... [they have] destroyed all balances and counterpoises which serve to fix a state and give it a steady direction, and then they melted down the whole into one incongruous mass of mob and democracy.⁶

Burke's speech before Parliament occurred on February 9, 1790, with its publication in America coinciding almost precisely with the appearance of John Adams' first *Davila* essay. And in November of that year, Burke expanded on his views in a lengthy pamphlet entitled *Reflections on the Revolution in France*.

Edmund Burke's *Reflections* completely incensed the British supporters of the French Revolution, sparking what has since become known as the "Revolution Controversy." As Burke had risen to refute Dr. Price and to disparage the Revolution, several writers angrily arose to hail the Revolution, and to refute Burke. The most prominent among these was Thomas Paine, author of *Common Sense*, the 1776 pamphlet that had so effectively rallied the American people against their king. To counter Burke's *Reflections*, Paine quickly penned *The Rights of Man*, a pamphlet which, while extolling the revolution in France, also openly derided the government of Great Britain.

Published in Europe in March of 1791, when *The Rights of Man* reached America, a copy fell into the hands of James Madison, who then passed it along to Thomas Jefferson. Being an ardent supporter of the revolution in France, Jefferson read *The Rights of Man* with great interest. And as he had been asked to do, Jefferson brought his copy of *The Rights of Man* to a Philadelphia printer, enclosing a letter which expressed his personal views of the work:

> He is extremely pleased to find that it will be re-printed here, and that something is at length to be publicly said against the political heresies which have sprung up among us. I have no doubt our citizens will rally a second time round the standard of *Common Sense*.[7]

The "political heresies" to which Jefferson referred, were, of course, John Adams' *Davila* essays, which after a year of publication, had just recently come to a close. The printer, seeing an opportunity to associate such an illustrious name with his publication, without Jefferson's permission or knowledge, added these endorsing statements as a preface to the first American printing of Thomas Paine's *The Rights of Man*.

Jefferson's apparent "endorsement" of Paine's views caused quite a stir within the Washington administration, for Jefferson was, at the time, serving as Washington's secretary of state. As the first president under a new constitution, Washington was attempting to cultivate and maintain both diplomatic and trade relations with the powers of Europe, and also to remain neutral regarding their disputes, especially those between the two great rivals, Britain and France. An "endorsement" of *The Rights of Man* and its ideas, coming from the American Secretary of State, threw a wrench into the diplomatic works, so to speak.

And the wording of Jefferson's "endorsement" also caused a rift between himself and Vice-President John Adams. Jefferson and Adams had been close friends since the early days of the American Revolution, and Jefferson had essentially called his old friend a political heretic.

Quarrels over the French Revolution were causing political lines to be drawn in America, with opposing views leading to factions and inevitably to political parties. And the first standard-bearers of the rising two political parties would be, John Adams and Thomas Jefferson.

It is in this context and political atmosphere that the letters of *Publicola* first appeared in print. For just as Edmund Burke had risen to respond to Dr. Price, and Thomas Paine had risen to respond to Edmund Burke, there now arose a figure to respond to Thomas Paine, and more subtly, to Thomas Jefferson.

Like the *Davila* essays, the letters of *Publicola* were published anonymously, and it was first thought that John Adams had once again taken up his pen, to defend himself against Jefferson's charge of "heresy." But more discerning readers of *Publicola* noted that, while the style of writing was similar to that of *Davila*, it was far more disciplined than that of the vice-president. *Publicola*, therefore, was indeed an Adams, but a different one, and it was soon revealed that it was John Quincy, and not John, who had authored the letters, to both defend his father and to respond to Paine and Jefferson.

At age twenty-three, John Quincy Adams dared to debate not only the most prominent men of the time, but also the most contentious issue of the time. And in doing so, he took his first step onto the world stage, for *Publicola* was very well received in Europe, with prominent members of the British Parliament claiming the letters to be "the best thing that has been written, and as one of the best pieces of reasoning and style they had ever read."[8]

However, subsequent events in France would quickly bring to an end any reasoned debate on the French Revolution. Edmund Burke and John Adams would prove to be eerily prescient, while their detractors, Paine and Jefferson, would prove to be disastrously wrong. For indeed the fate of France would soon be one of anarchy, tyranny and blood, followed by dictatorship and war – war which would persist for over twenty years.

But in June of 1791, as the letters of *Publicola* first appeared in the papers, that fate was, as yet, unknown.

LETTER I.

June 8, 1791

Mr. Russell,

Sir, The late Revolution in France has opened an extensive field of speculation to the philosopher and to the politician. An event so astonishing and unexpected in its nature, and so important in its consequences, naturally arrested the peculiar attention of the whole civilized world. The friends of liberty, and of man have seen with pleasure the temples of despotism levelled with the ground, and the Genius of Freedom, rising suddenly, in his collected and irresistible strength, and snapping in an instant all the cords with which, for centuries, he had been bound. Upon the downfall of the arbitrary system of government in France, there appears to have been but one sentiment, and that, a sentiment of exultation; but while the friends of humanity have rejoiced at the emancipation of so many millions of their fellow creatures, they have waited with an anxious expectation to see upon what foundations they would attempt to establish their newly acquired liberty. The proceedings of their Representative Assembly have been contemplated in very different points of view, by men of names equally illustrious, and of characters equally favorable to the cause of liberty. Among the publications which have appeared upon the subject, two pamphlets, founded upon very different principles, appear to have been received with the greatest avidity, and seem calculated to leave the deepest impression.[1] The one, written by Mr. Burke, which is one continued invective upon almost all the proceedings of the National Assembly since the Revolution, and which passes a severe and indiscriminating censure upon almost all their transactions; the other, the production of Mr. Paine, containing a defense of the Assembly, and approving everything they have done, with applause as undistinguishing as is the censure of Mr. Burke. We are told, that the copy from which an edition of this work was reprinted at Philadelphia, was furnished by the Secretary of State, and was accompanied by a letter, from which the following extract has been published in most of our newspapers: "I am extremely pleased to find that it is to be re-printed here, and that something is at length to be publicly said against the *political heresies* which have sprung up among us. I have no doubt our citizens will *rally* a second time round the standard of *Common Sense.*"

I confess, Sir, I am somewhat at a loss to determine, what this very respectable gentleman means by *political heresies.* Does he consider this pamphlet of Mr. Paine's as the canonical book of political scripture? As containing the true doctrine of popular infallibility, from which it would be heretical to depart in one single point? The expressions, indeed, imply more; they seem, like the Arabian

---

[1] *Reflections on the Revolution in France* by Edmund Burke and *The Rights of man* by Thomas Paine

prophet, to call upon all true believers in the *Islam* of democracy, to draw their swords, and, in the fervor of their devotion, to compel all their countrymen to cry out: "There is but one Goddess of Liberty, and *Common Sense* is her prophet."

I have always understood, Sir, that the citizens of these States were possessed of a full and entire freedom of opinion upon all subjects, civil as well as religious; they have not yet established any infallible criterion of *orthodoxy,* either in church or state; their principles in theory, and their habits in practice, are equally averse to that slavery of the mind, which adopts, without examination, any sentiment that has the sanction of a venerable name. *Nullius in verba jurara magistri*[2] is their favorite maxim; and the only political tenet which they would stigmatize with the name of heresy, would be that which should attempt to impose an opinion upon their understandings, upon the single principle of authority.

I believe also, Sir, that the citizens of America are not at present disposed to rally round the standard of any man. In the full possession and enjoyment of all the freedom for which they have gone through so arduous a conflict,[3] they will not, for the poor purpose of extinguishing a few supposed political heresies, return to the horrors of a civil contest from which they could reap no possible benefit, and which would probably terminate in the loss of that liberty, for which they have been so liberal of their treasure and of their blood.

---

[2] Trust no authority
[3] The recent American Revolution

If, however, Mr. Paine is to be adopted as the holy father of our political faith, and this pamphlet is to be considered as his Papal Bull of infallible virtue, let us at least examine what it contains. Before we determine to join the standard, let us inquire what are the articles of war, to which our General requires our submission. It is the glorious characteristic of truth, at once to invite and bid defiance to investigation. If any opinions which have sprung up among us have really led us astray from the standard of *truth*, let us return to it, at the call of Mr. Paine, or of any other man who can show us our errors. But, Sir, if, upon examination, even this testament of orthodoxy shall be found to contain many spurious texts, false in their principles and delusive in their inferences, we may be permitted, notwithstanding our reverence for the author, at least to expunge the apocryphal doctrine, and to confine our faith to the genuine tenets of real political inspiration. It is my intention to submit to the public, a few observations which have occurred to me upon the perusal of this pamphlet which has so clear and valid a title to the public attention. But I must here observe that I wish to avoid every appearance of disrespect, either to the real parent of this production, or to the gentleman who has stood its sponsor in this country. Both these gentlemen are entitled to the gratitude of their countrymen; the latter still renders important services in a very dignified station. He is a friend to free inquiry upon every subject, and he will not be displeased to see the sentiments which he has made his own by a public adoption, canvassed with as much freedom as is consistent with the reverence due his character.

LETTER II.

June 11, 1791

Sir, In that part of Mr. Paine's pamphlet which he has chosen to call the miscellaneous chapter, he observes that, "when a man in a long cause attempts to steer his course by anything else than some *polar truth or principle*, he is sure to be lost." I have sought for the polar principle to which his exertions were directed in this publication, and I must acknowledge I have sought in vain. His production is historical, political, miscellaneous, satirical and panegyrical. It is an encomium upon the National Assembly of France. It is a commentary upon the rights of man, inferring questionable deductions from unquestionable principles. It is a severe satire upon Mr. Burke and his pamphlet upon the English Government, upon Kings, upon Nobility, and Aristocracy; it is a narrative of several occurrences, connected with the French Revolution, and it concludes with a kind of prophetical impulse, in the expectation of an "*European Congress to patronize the progress of free government, and promote the civilization of nations with each other.*" The object which he promised to himself in this publication, is not so dubious as the principle on which he wrote. His intention appears evidently to be, to convince the people of Great Britain that they have neither Liberty nor a Constitution — that their only possible means to produce these blessings to themselves is to "topple-down headlong," their present government, and follow implicitly the example of the French. As to the right, he scruples not to say, "that which a whole nation chooses to do, it has a right to do." This proposition is a part of what Mr. Paine calls, a system of principles in opposition to those of Mr. Burke, and it is laid down without any sort of qualification. It is not my intention to defend the principles of Mr. Burke; truth is the only object of my pursuit, and I shall without hesitation refuse my assent to every principle inconsistent with that, whether it proceeds from Mr. Burke, Mr. Paine, or even from the illustrious National Assembly of France. This principle, that a whole nation has a right to do whatever it pleases, cannot in any sense whatever be admitted as true. The eternal and immutable laws of justice and of morality are paramount to all human legislation. The violation of those laws is certainly within the power, but it is not among the rights of nations. The power of a nation is the collected power of all the individuals which compose it. The rights of a nation are in like manner, the collected rights of its individuals; and it must *follow* from thence, that the powers of a nation are more extensive than its rights, in the very same proportion with those of individuals. It is somewhat remarkable that, in speaking of the exercise of the particular right of forming a Constitution, Mr. Paine himself denies to a nation that omnipotence which he had before so liberally bestowed. For this same nation, which has a right to do whatever it pleases, has no right to establish a Government in *heredi-*

tary succession. It is of infinite consequence, that the distinction between *power* and *right* should be fully acknowledged, and admitted as one of the fundamental principles of Legislators. A whole nation, such as France, England, or America, can act only by representation; and the acts of the representative body must be considered as the acts of the nation. We must go farther and say, that the acts of the majority in the Representative Assembly are the acts of the whole body, and consequently of the whole nation. If, therefore, a majority thus constituted are bound by no law, human or divine, and have no other rule but their sovereign will and pleasure to direct them, what possible security can any citizen of the nation have for the protection of his unalienable rights? The principles of liberty must still be the sport of arbitrary power, and the hideous form of despotism must lay aside the diadem and the scepter, only to assume the party-colored garments of democracy.

The system of principles upon which Mr. Paine advances this assertion is intended to prove that the English nation have a right to destroy their present form of Government, and to erect another. I am not disposed to deny this right, nor is it at present necessary to examine whether Mr. Burke's opinions upon this subject are not directed rather against the expediency than the abstracted rights of such a measure. It may, however, not be improper to trace the origin of Mr. Paine's arguments against the principles maintained by Mr. Burke. Dr. Price[4] has asserted, that by "the principles of the Revolution in 1688, the people of England had acquired the right, 1. To choose their own Governors; 2. To cashier them for misconduct; and 3. To frame a Government for themselves." Mr. Burke endeavors to prove that the principles of the Revolution in 1688, so far from warranting any right of this kind, support a doctrine almost diametrically opposite. Mr. Paine, in reply, cuts the Gordian knot at once, declares the Parliament of 1688 to have been downright usurpers, censures them for having unwisely sent to Holland for a King; denies the existence of a British Constitution, and invites the people of England to overturn their present Government, and to erect another upon the broad basis of national sovereignty, and government by representation. As Mr. Paine has departed altogether from the principles of the Revolution, and has torn up by the roots all reasoning from the British Constitution, by the denial of its existence, it becomes necessary to examine his works upon the grounds which he has chosen to assume. If we judge of the production from its apparent tendency, we may call it an address to the English nation, attempting to prove that they have a right to form a new Constitution; that it is expedient for them immediately to exercise that right; and that, in the formation of this Constitution, they can do no better than to imitate the model set before them by the French National Assembly. However immethodical his

---

[4] Dr. Richard Price, whose 1789 sermon, *A Discourse on the Love of our Country*, had compared the revolution in France to England's Glorious Revolution of 1688, prompting Burke to pen his *Reflections*

production is, I believe the whole of its argumentative part may be referred to these three points. If the subject were to affect only the British nation, we might leave them to reason and act for themselves; but, Sir, these are concerns equally important to all mankind; and the citizens of America are called upon from high authority, to *rally* round the *standard* of this champion of Revolutions. I shall therefore now proceed to examine the reasons upon which he founds his opinions relative to each of these points.

The people of England have, in common with other nations, a natural and unalienable right to form a Constitution of Government, not because a whole nation has a right to do whatever it chooses to do, but because Government, being instituted for the common security of the natural rights of every individual, it must be liable to alterations whenever it becomes incompetent for that purpose. The right of the people to legislate for succeeding generations derives all its authority from the consent of that posterity who are bound by their laws; and therefore the expressions of perpetuity used by the Parliament of 1688 contain no absurdity; and expressions of a similar nature may be found in all the Constitutions of the United States.

But, Sir, when this right is thus admitted in its fullest latitude, it must also be admitted, that it ought never to be exercised but in cases of extreme urgency: Every nation has a right, as unquestionable, to dissolve the bands of civil society by which they are united, and to return to that state of individual imbecility in which man is supposed to have existed, previous to the formation of the social compact. The people of America have been compelled, by an unaccountable necessity, distressing in its operation, but glorious in its consequences, to exercise this right; and whenever a nation has no other alternative but the degradation of slavery, or the formidable conflict of a Revolution, the generous spirit of freedom will not hesitate a moment in the choice. Whether the people of France were, at the period of their Revolution, reduced to that unhappy situation, which rendered it absolutely necessary to overthrow their whole system to its foundations, is a question upon which the ablest patriots among themselves have differed, and upon which we are inadequate to decide. Whether the people of England are now in the calamitous predicament, is a question more proper for our discussion, and upon which I shall take the liberty to examine the reasoning of Mr. Paine.

LETTER III.

June 15, 1791

Sir, In examining the question whether the English nation have a right, fundamentally, to demolish their present form of government, it becomes necessary to inquire, whether Mr. Paine's assertion that there is no such thing as an English Constitution, be really true? This question may perhaps, in some measure, affect the people of America. For if the government of Great Britain is an usurpation, it may be worthy of consideration how far we are bound by treaties which do not reciprocally bind the inhabitants of that island?

"A Constitution," says Mr. Paine, "is not a thing in name only, but in fact. It has not an ideal, but a real existence; and wherever it cannot be produced in a visible form, there is none." Mr. Paine should have gone farther, and told us whether, like a deed, it must be written on paper or parchment, or whether it has a larger latitude, and may be engraved on stone, or carved in wood. From the tenor of his argument, it should seem that he had only the American Constitutions in his mind, for excepting them, I believe he would not find in all history, a government which will come within his definition; and, of course, there never was a people that had a Constitution previous to the year 1776. But the word, with an idea affixed to it, had been in use, and commonly understood, for centuries before that period; and therefore Mr. Paine must, to suit his purpose, alter its acceptations, and, in the warmth of his zeal for Revolutions, endeavor to bring about a revolution in language also. When all the most illustrious Whig writers in England have contended for the liberty of their country upon the principles of the English Constitution; when the glorious Congress of 1774 declared, that "the inhabitants of the English colonies in North America were entitled to certain rights by the immutable laws of nature, *the principles of the English Constitution,* and the several charters of compacts," they knew very well what they meant, and were perfectly understood by all mankind. Mr. Paine says, that "a Constitution is to a Government, what the laws, made afterwards by that Government, are to a court of judicature." But, when the American States, by their Constitutions, expressly adopted the whole body of the *common law,* so far as it was applicable to their respective situations, did they adopt nothing at all, because that law cannot be produced in a visible form? No, Sir, the Constitution of a country is not the paper or parchment upon which the compact is written, it is the system of fundamental laws by which the people have consented to be governed, which is always supposed to be impressed upon the mind of every individual, and of which the written or printed copies are nothing more than the evidence.

In this sense, Sir, the British nation have a Constitution, which was for many years the admiration of the world; the people of America, with very good reason, have renounced some of its defects and infirmities. But in defense of some of its principles, they have fought and conquered. It is composed of a venerable *system* of unwritten or customary laws, handed down from time immemorial, and sanctioned by the accumulated experience of ages; and of a body of statutes, enacted by an authority lawfully competent to that purpose. Mr. Paine is certainly mistaken, when he considers the British government as having originated in the conquest of William of Normandy. This principle of being governed by an oral or traditionary law prevailed in England eleven hundred years before that invasion. It has continued to this day, and has been adopted by all the American States. I hope they will never abolish a system so excellent, merely because it cannot be produced in a visible form. The Constitution of Great Britain is a Constitution of *principles,* not of *articles,* and however frequently it may have been violated by tyrants, monarchical, aristocratical, or democratical, the people have always found it expedient to restore the original foundations, while from time to time they have been successful in improving and ornamenting the building.

The people of England are bound, therefore, by a social compact now existing; and they have no right to demolish their Government, unless it be clearly incompetent for the purposes for which it was instituted. They have delegated their whole collective power to a Legislature, consisting of a King, Lords, and Commons, and they have included even the power of altering the Constitution itself. Should they abuse this power so that the nation itself should be oppressed, and their rights to life, liberty, and property, instead of protection, should meet with tyranny, the people would certainly be entitled to appeal, in the last resort, to themselves, to resume the trust which has been so unworthily betrayed, and (not to do whatever they should choose, but) to form another Constitution, which should more permanently secure the natural rights of the whole community. The same may be said of the National Assembly of France, who, according to Mr. Paine's idea, are possessed of the whole collective power of the nation, and who seem, like him, to think they have a right to do whatever they choose. Mr. Paine says, that "the authority of the present Assembly is different to what the authority of future Assemblies will be." But if the present Assembly should decree that all future National Assemblies should possess the same power with themselves, it would certainly be binding as an article of the Constitution. Mr. Paine, indeed, will not acknowledge this; and it is the second right which he denies his nation, which, at the same time, has a right to do everything. Mr. Paine's ideas upon this subject appear to have been formed by a partial adoption of the principle upon which Rousseau founds the social compact. But neither the principle of Rousseau, nor that of Mr. Paine, is true. Rousseau contends that the social compact is formed by a personal association of individuals, which must be unanimously assented to, and which cannot possibly be made by a representative body. I shall not at present spend much of my time in showing that this is neither practicable nor even metaphysically true. I shall only observe, that its operation would annihilate, in an instant, all the power of the National Assembly, and turn the whole body of the American Constitutions (the pride of man, the glory of the human understanding) into a mass of tyrannical and unfounded usurpations. Mr. Paine does not go quite so far, but we must examine whether his arguments are not equally wide from the truth. "A government," says he, "on the principles on which Constitutional Governments, arising out of society, are established, cannot have the right of altering itself. Why not? Because if it had, it would be arbitrary." But this reason is not sufficient. A nation, in forming a social compact, may delegate the whole of their collective powers to ordinary legislatures, in perpetual succession, and reserve only the right of resisting the abuse of those powers; and every other question relative to the reservation of powers to the nation, must be only a questions of expediency. The same power which the present National Assembly possess in France, is, by the English Constitution, constantly vested in the King and Parliament of Great Britain; and the people in both kingdoms have the same right to resist and punish the abuse of that power.

Surely, Sir, the people of the Unites States have a Constitution, although they have given the power of making alterations, to those by whom it is administered, in conjunction with the State Legislatures. Surely, the people of Massachusetts have a Constitution, though it provides for certain alterations by the ordinary Legislatures, and though, since it was formed, such alterations have accordingly been made. The Constitutions of several of the United States are expressly made alterable in every part by their ordinary Legislatures. I think there is not one of them, but admits of alterations without recurring to "the nation in its original character." Yet Mr. Paine will surely acknowledge, that the American Constitutions arose out of the people, and not over them. His principle, therefore, "that a Constitutional Government cannot have the right of altering itself," is not true. In forming their Constitutions, a nation may reserve to themselves such powers as they think proper. They may reserve only the unalienable right of resistance against tyranny. The people of England have reserved only this right. The French National Assembly have been in session more than two years, to make laws nominally paramount to their future Legislatures. I shall hazard some observations upon this subject, when I attempt to follow Mr. Paine, through his comparison between the French and English Constitutions. But as the English have delegated all their power, I contend they have no right in their original character to change their form of Government, unless it has become incompetent for the purposes for which all Governments are instituted. I am aware of the question which will occur here. Who is to judge of this incompetency? And I am aware of the triumphant manner in which it may be asked. But a triumph is not my object, and in the pursuit of truth I shall venture in my next number to consider this subject.

LETTER IV.

June 18, 1791

Sir, I have assumed for a principle, that the English nation, having delegated all their collective power, have no right in their original character, to change their form of Government, unless it has become absolutely inadequate to the purposes for which it was instituted. The people themselves, must from the necessity of the case be the judges of this fact; but if in forming this judgment, and acting in pursuance of it, they proceed from passion, and not from principle; if they dissolve their compact, from an idea that "they have a right to do whatever they choose," and break the bands of society, in the forms of despotism, "because such is their pleasure," they may indeed go through the operation by the plenitude of their irresistible power; but the nation will meet with ample punishment in their own misery, and the leaders who delude them, in the detestation of their own posterity. It is not by adopting the malignity of a political satirist, by converting the sallies of wit into the maxims of truth or justice, or by magnifying trivial imperfections into capital crimes, that a nation will be justified in resorting to its original strength, to contend against its delegated power. It is not a mechanical horror against the name of a king, or of aristocracy, nor a physical antipathy to the sound of an extravagant title, or to the sight of an innocent ribband, that can authorize a people to lay violent hands upon the Constitution, which protects their rights, and guards their liberties. They must feel an actual deprivation of their equal rights, and see an actual impossibility for their restoration in any other manner, before they can have a right to lay their hands on their swords, and appeal to heaven. These are not the principles of slavery; they are the tenets of the only genuine liberty, which consists in a mean equally distant from the despotism of an individual, as of a million. They are sanctioned by our own uniform example, and will, I trust, never be departed from by the most enlightened, and most virtuous people on the globe. For sixteen years the people of America endured a continual succession of every indignity, which the pride of dominion, the insolence of power, and the rapacity of avarice, could inflict upon them, before they could resolve to renounce an authority, three thousand miles distant from them; and even then, they were so far from thinking they had a right to do whatever they chose; that by the very act which renounced their connection with Great Britain they exposed to the world their own sufferings, and the various acts of tyranny, which had compelled them to "acquiesce in the necessity which denounced the separation," and, "appealed to the Supreme Judge of the world for the rectitude of their intentions." No, Sir, the venerable character who drew up this declaration never could believe that the rights of a nation, have no other limits, than its powers. Since the Revolution, the people of the United States have again been compelled to form a national Government, and in its formation proceeded in the same spirit. The confederation[5] was found totally incompetent for the purposes for which it was instituted; not from an abuse of the delegated powers, in those by whom it was administered, but because scarcely any powers at all had been given. The inefficiency of that system had long been fully demonstrated, and had reduced us to extreme distress. The States, united but in name, were upon the verge of general bankruptcy. Their credit, sunk to the lowest ebb, was upon the point of expiring, and their exhausted treasury gave perpetually the lie to their public faith, so often and so solemnly pledged. The forcible ties of a common interest, directed to one great object during the war, were greatly loosened by the accomplishment of that object, and the seeds of mutual hostility were sown by the partial commercial regulations of the respective States. The revenue laws which had been enacted in several of the States were not able to support their credit, and yet were so unequal in their operation, that numerous bodies of men, in more than one of the States, appeared in open rebellion against the mildest Governments that ever were instituted. Instead of the glorious reward which the people had expected for their virtuous exertions, internal discord, and infamy abroad presented themselves in dreary perspective before them. At that critical period, when the system to be annihilated, was an empty name, and there was only a Government to be formed, the national Constitution was

---

[5] The loose gathering of the thirteen American colonies under the Articles of Confederation

presented to the people of America "in their original character;" and even then its existence was to depend upon the assent of nine States, that is, two thirds of the people. Very fortunately it has at length been freely adopted by all the members of the Union; but the extreme difficulty which impeded the progress of its adoption, and the various amendments,[6] which in many of the States, were, in a manner, made the condition of their assent, exhibit the fullest evidence, what a more than Herculean task it is, to unite the opinions of a free people, upon any system of government whatever.

Under the sanction of such authority, I venture to assert, that the people of England have no right to destroy their government, unless in its operation the rights of the people are really oppressed, and unless they have attempted in vain every constitutional mode of obtaining redress. These principles ought to operate with peculiar force upon the people of England, because, in the uncertain and hazardous event of a Revolution, they have more to lose and less to gain, than any other European nation, and because whatever they acquire, must, in all probability be purchased at the expense of a civil war. When provision is made for the alteration of a constitution, otherwise than by the common legislative power, it may be done comparatively without difficulty or danger; but where this power is already delegated, with the other powers of legislation, the people cannot use it themselves, except in their original, individual, unrepresented character, and they cannot acquire the right to act in that capacity, until

---

[6] The Bill of Rights

the power which they have thus conveyed in trust has been abdicated by the extreme abuses of its administration.

When Mr. Paine invited the people of England to destroy their present Government, and form another Constitution, he should have given them sober reasoning, and not flippant witticisms. He should have explained to them the nature of the grievances by which they are oppressed, and demonstrated the impossibility of reforming the Government in its present organization. He should have pointed out to them some possible method for them to act in their original character, without a total dissolution of civil society among them; he should have proved what great advantages they would reap, as a nation, from such a revolution, without disguising the great dangers and formidable difficulties with which it must be attended.

The principal and most dangerous abuses in the English Government, arise less from the defects inherent in the Constitution, than from the state of society; the universal venality and corruption which pervades all classes of men in that kingdom, and which a change of government could not reform. I shall consider this subject more largely hereafter; but at present, with respect to the expediency of a revolution in England, I must inquire how the nation can be brought to act in their original character? Mr. Paine, perhaps from delicacy of his situation, has said nothing openly upon this very important point. Yet, in two different parts of his work, he seems obscurely to hint two methods for the accomplishment of this object. When he compares the situation of the citizens of London to that of the inhabitants of Paris just before the taking of the Bastille,[7] it seems as if it was with an intention to recommend a similar insurrection for the purpose of dispensing the Parliament, and expelling the King, which would leave the nation without any government at all, and compel them at all events to act in their original character. When he advises "Revolutions by accommodation," he must probably mean that a convention should be called by act of Parliament to regenerate their Constitution. I cannot imagine any other method of answering his purpose. Mr. Paine seems to think it is as easy for a nation to change its government, as for a man to change his coat; but, I confess, both the modes of proceeding which he suggests, appear to me to be liable to great objections.

---

[7] July 14, 1789

LETTER V.

June 22, 1791

Sir, "There are in all European countries," says Mr. Paine, "a large class of people of that description, which in England are called the *mob.*" It was by the people of this description that the Bastille in Paris was destroyed. In London there is no Bastille to demolish; but there is a government to overturn; and there is a King and Parliament, who must either be put to flight, or compelled to call a convention for the purpose of forming a Constitution. "In the commencement of a Revolution, those men are rather the followers of the *camp* than of the *standard* of liberty, and have yet to be instructed how to reverence it." As these men were made instrumental to the accomplishment of the Revolution in France, Mr. Paine appears to intimate, that they may be employed for a similar purpose in England. I am as little disposed as Mr. Paine can be, to reproach either the whole nation to which they belong, or that unhappy class of human beings themselves, for the devastation which they commit. They cannot be considered as free agents, and therefore are neither the subjects of praise or blame; but the friend of humanity will be extremely cautious how he ventures to put in action a tremendous power, which is competent only to the purposes of destruction, and totally incapable either to create or to preserve. This class of men, of whom it is the happiness of Americans scarcely to be able to form an idea, can be brought to act in concert upon no other principles than those of a frantic enthusiasm and ungovernable fury; their profound ignorance and deplorable credulity make them proper tools for any man who can inflame their passions, or alarm their superstition; and as they have nothing to lose by the total dissolution of civil society, their rage may be easily directed against any victim which may be pointed out to them. They are altogether incapable of forming a rational judgment, either upon the principles or the motives of their own conduct; and whether the object for which they are made to contend be good or bad, the brutal arm of power is all the assistance they can afford for its accomplishment. To set in motion this inert mass, the eccentric vivacity of a madman is infinitely better calculated than the sober coolness of phlegmatic reason. They need only to be provoked and irritated, and they never can in any other manner be called into action. In the year 1780, they assembled at London, to the number of 60,000, under the direction of Lord George Gordon, and carrying fire and slaughter before them, were upon the point of giving the whole city of London to one undistinguished devastation and destruction; and this, because the Parliament had mitigated the severity of a sanguinary and tyrannical law of persecution against the Roman Catholics. Should these people be taught that they have a right to do everything, and that the titles of Kings and Nobles, and the wealth of Bishops, are all usurpations and robberies committed upon them, I believe it would not be difficult to rouse their passions, and to prepare them for every work of ruin and destruction. But, Sir, when they are once put in motion, they soon get beyond all restraint and control. The rights of man to life, liberty, and property, oppose but a feeble barrier to them; the beauteous face of nature, and the elegant refinements of art, the hoary head of wisdom, and the enchanting smile of beauty, are all equally liable to become obnoxious to them; and as all their power consists in destruction, whatever meets with their displeasure must be devoted to ruin. Could anything but an imperious, overruling necessity, justify any man or body of men, for using a weapon like this to operate a Revolution in Government? Such, indeed, was the situation of the French National Assembly when they directed the electric fluid of this popular frenzy against the ancient fabric of their monarchy. They justly thought that no price could purchase too dearly the fall of arbitrary power in an individual; but perhaps even *they* were not aware of all the consequences which might follow from committing the existence of the kingdom to the custody of a lawless and desperate rabble.

But do the people of England labor under such intolerable oppression as would authorize any of their patriots to employ an arm like this for their relief? Suppose sixty thousand men should again assemble round Westminster Hall, and with clubs and fire-brands for their sole arguments, should compel the Parliament to call a convention to make a Constitution, what would be the probable consequences? Is it clear that so large a majority of the people of England have lost all their attachment to their Constitution, as to insure an acquiescence in the measure throughout the kingdom? Is it certain that one quarter part of the people would obey an act extorted by such violence as that? Would not all the friends of the present Government rally round the standard of the Constitution, and would not their duty compel them to defend it with their lives and fortunes? If it should soon appear that they were decidedly the strongest party, would not the insurrection be extinguished in the blood of its leaders? If the parties should prove to be nearly equal, would not the nation be involved in all the horrors of a long and bloody civil war? In whatever point of view the effects of this scheme are contemplated, they present nothing but prospects at which every friend of mankind must shudder; nor can I possibly believe that Mr. Paine, who is certainly a benevolent man, would deliberately recommend this method, though in his ardent zeal for the honor of the French nation, and the propagation of their doctrine, he has incautiously suggested it.

But he recommends Revolutions by accommodation, which applied to England, must mean, that a convention be called by a free and deliberate act of Parliament, to alter the Constitution; but this plan appears to be equally dangerous with the other, and more impracticable; while by a singular fatality an act of this kind would be the completest evidence of its own inutility, it would be equally dangerous, because, by a formal act of competent authority, it would expose the kingdom to all the evils of anarchy and of war, which in the other case would result from a popular convulsion. It would be less practicable, because it is contrary to nature, that any body of men should venture to perform the most transcendent act of power of which human beings are capable, for the single purpose of divesting themselves of all power whatever. It would prove its own inutility, because no man will presume that they ought to take such a measure, unless the wishes of a clear and decided majority of the people are favorable to an alteration of the Government. If they are disposed to act in conformity with the desires of the people, the very same power which would authorize them to dissolve the Government, would likewise justify them in making any alterations which should meet with the wishes of the nation, and would render a recurrence to them, "in their original character," perfectly unnecessary.

Whatever Mr. Paine's opinion may be with respect to the existence of an English Constitution, it is certain that every member of the British Parliament, who gives his vote in the making of a new law, or the alteration of an old one, must suppose that he acts by virtue of a Constitutional right vested in him; but the same right which authorizes him to give his suffrage on the most trifling object of legislation, has vested in the Parliament, of which he is a member, the whole power of the British nation, and he cannot possibly deny their right, without utterly destroying his own. The right of the individual depends altogether upon the right of the corporation, and his right to vote for the regulation of a turnpike, or the toll of a bridge, is the same with theirs to make every necessary and convenient alteration in the Constitution of the kingdom itself. While they are thus convinced of their right to exercise these great powers, would it not be the summit of extravagance and folly in them; nay, would it not be the most flagrant breach of the trust reposed in them, of which they could possibly be guilty, to abdicate an authority lawfully committed to them, to declare themselves altogether incompetent to a wise and prudent use of a Constitutional power, and to commit the peace, the welfare, the very existence of the nation, to the uncertain and hazardous event of a Revolution?

If, however, we can suppose that the Parliament should finally accede to the idea, that they are mere tyrants, without the shadow of a right to the authority which they have hitherto exercised, the only act which they could agree to would be a vote to dissolve themselves, and leave the vessel of the state without either a pilot or a rudder. For the very act of calling a convention would be an usurpation, and from the importance of its consequences, an usurpation of the most daring nature: it would be assuming the right to dissolve the ties of society, and at the same instant acknowledging that this assumed right was without any sort of foundation. In short, this plan of calling a convention to alter the Constitution, by act of Parliament, appears to me, in whatever light it is considered, to involve an absurdity.

But, as there is unquestionably somewhere in England, a combination of the right and of the power to alter the Constitution of the country, and as that Constitution is indubitably liable to be improved, we may be permitted to inquire, whether a blind imitation of the French National Assembly would probably promote the happiness of the people; the only object for which all Governments were instituted, or which can authorize their alteration.

LETTER VI.

June 29, 1791

Sir, Mr. Paine affirms that the French nation have a Constitution, and that the English have none. I have already offered a few observations upon the latter part of this assertion; but, as a preliminary to some remarks, which I propose to make upon his comparison, I must premise, that directly the reverse of his opinion upon this subject is the truth, and that in reality the English nation have a Constitution, and the French as yet have none. The National Assembly have indeed been constantly sitting these two years, to form a Constitution; and at the ceremony of the Federation, about eleven months since, they swore themselves and their King to the observance of a Constitution *to be made.* But as they are still possessed of the whole power of the nation, they may repeal any article upon which they have hitherto agreed, by virtue of the same authority which enabled them to pass the decree, and therefore, according to Mr. Paine's own ideas, the French cannot be said to have a Constitution, until the National Assembly shall please to dissolve themselves, and to put their whole system into full operation.

I have endeavored to show, that it is not absolutely essential to the existence of a Constitution, that is should be producible "in a visible form." The period of time when the foundations of the present English government were laid, by the association of the people in "their original character," cannot indeed be ascertained. Many of the laws which are in use to this day in Great Britain, and from thence have been adopted by the American Republics, may be traced back to the remotest period of antiquity; and the origin even of the institution of Juries, an institution so congenial to the genuine spirit of freedom, is lost in the obscurity of the fabulous ages. Many of the fundamental principles of the English Constitution are known to have existed long before the invention of printing, and even before the inhabitants of Britain were acquainted with the use of letters, and it would therefore be an absurdity to require that the original articles should be produced "in a visible form." But, "*ex nihilo nihil fit,*"[8] the very existence of these principles proves the formation of a social compact previous to that existence; and that spirit of liberty, which is their distinguishing characteristic, affords internal evidence, that they did not originate in the merciless despotism of a conqueror, but in the free and unrestrained consent of a manly and generous people. It will not be said that an original compact was never formed, because it is not recorded in the page of history; as well might it be pretended that the pyramids of Egypt arose self-created from the earth, because the time of their erection, and the names of their builders, have been consigned to that oblivion, in which all human labors are destined to be overwhelmed.

---

[8] Out of nothing comes nothing

William of Normandy, to whom Mr. Paine always refers the origin of the English government, was the conqueror only of Harold. He obtained the crown of England by popular election, upon the express condition that he would govern the nation according to her ancient laws and customs; he took the same oath at his coronation which had been taken by his predecessors, and by his last will, after bequeathing the province of Normandy to his eldest son Robert, he expressly acknowledged that he did not possess the kingdom of England as an inheritance, and only recommended his son William as his successor. It would be altogether unnecessary at this time to discuss the question, whether the crown of England was originally hereditary or elective, but the facts which I have stated, and which are warranted by all the most ancient and most authentic English historians, fully demonstrate that the English government did not originate in the Norman Conquest. "If the succession runs in the line of the conquest, *the nation,* runs in the line of being conquered, and it ought to rescue itself from this reproach," says Mr. Paine. "The victory obtained at Hastings not being a victory over *the nation collectively,* but only over the person of Harold, the only right that the conqueror could pretend to acquire thereby, was the right to possess the crown of England, not *to alter the nature of the Government"* says Judge Blackstone (I Comm. 199). Upon a question of fact relative to the English Constitution, Blackstone is, I believe, as good an authority as Mr. Paine, but I wish not to rest the question upon any authority whatever: I venture to affirm, that any man who will coolly and impartially examine the subject, and appeal to the original sources of information, will acknowledge, that those who derive the origin of the English Government from William the Conqueror, can do it upon no other principle than that of supporting a system.

It is not, however, necessary upon the present occasion to revive a question, which has been discussed among the English with all the acrimony of faction. Mr. Paine has chosen the ground, which was not found tenable by the slavish supporters of passive obedience and the divine right of Kings. They took it originally, because it was necessary to them for the support of their system, and they were driven from it, by the friends and supporters of equal liberty. Mr. Paine found it necessary to support a doctrine of a very different nature; and, adopting the maxim that is lawful to learn, even from our enemies, he has freely borrowed from them the practice of accommodating the facts of history to his political purposes.

Be that, however, as it may, the Parliament of Great Britain, from time to time, have enacted certain laws, which, from their superior importance, have been denominated Constitutional; the acquiescence of the people, to whom most of those laws have been extremely satisfactory, gives them at least as good a sanction as the Constitution of France has obtained. The National Assembly were not originally chosen to form a Constitution. They were called together as States-General, under the authority of another Constitution, such as it was. They assumed the power to dissolve the old Constitution, and to form another, and the acquiescence of the people has confirmed that assumption. At all events, therefore, their Constitution stands upon no better ground than the acts of the British Parliament.

If, then, the Parliament of Great Britain have a right to declare what shall be the supreme law of the land, they will be able to produce a system of Constitutional law, even according to Mr. Paine's wish, "in a visible form." This system is contained in a number of statutes, enacted not at one time, or by one body of men, but at divers times, according to the occasional convenience of the people, and by a competent authority. These statutes contain the principles upon which the English Government is founded, and are therefore proper objects of comparison with the Constitution which is to be the supreme law of the land in France. The comparisons with Mr. Paine has drawn, are not partially favorable to his native country. We shall inquire whether they are perfectly consistent with the truth.

LETTER VII.

July 2, 1791

Sir, By the English Constitution, the whole collective power of the nation is delegated, and the Constitution itself is alterable by the same authority which is competent to the common purposes of legislation.

The French are to have a Constitution, every part of which will be nominally beyond the control of their common legislatures, and which will be unalterable in all parts, except by the nation in its "original character." At least Mr. Paine has undertaken to answer for them that it will be so: although I have not seen any such article in the Constitution, and though perhaps it has not yet been decreed, I am willing to take Mr. Paine's word for the fact, and to consider the subject as it were already determined.

I have made some observations upon Mr. Paine's arguments, as they respect the right of a nation to delegate all their power. As a question of expediency, it may perhaps be more difficult to determine which of these two schemes contains the least evil. Both of them are supported by the example of several among the American States, and can therefore boast the sanction of authorities equally respectable.

The fundamental principle upon which society is formed, appears to be, in order that the power of the whole may be rendered subservient to the interests of the whole. The problem to solve is, in what manner the power shall be distributed, so as most effectually to answer that purpose? Considering the extreme difficulty with which a whole nation can be brought to act in their original character, it should seem that wisdom must dictate to them the necessity of delegating their whole power, in such a manner as that it may be rendered beneficial to the nation, because whatever power is retained by the people, cannot be exercised for their advantage, any more than to their injury. The question therefore occurs, why a nation should not delegate all its powers? Mr. Paine has bestowed a very little consideration upon this subject; I find that although he gives his own opinion very freely, he offers only two reasons to support it. One, because "such a Government would be arbitrary;" the other, because "there is a paradox in the idea of vitiated bodies reforming themselves." In the sense in which the word arbitrary is here used, the first argument attacks the foundation of civil society itself; for whenever a number of individuals associate together, and form themselves into a body politic, called a nation, the possession and the use of the whole power (which is not, however, arbitrary power), is the very object of their association. This power must exist somewhere, and I cannot see the reason why it should not exist for the benefit of the people. But whenever a Constitution is made unalterable by the common legislative authority, the nation do in reality abdicate all the powers which they are said to retain, and declare that very important powers shall at all events be useless to them, from an apprehension that they might possibly be abused to their injury. It is as if a man should bind himself never to wear a sword, lest he should turn it against his own breast. The only reason why the whole power of a nation should not be delegated, must arise from the danger of its being abused. And a melancholy experience has always shown, that when the whole power has been thus delegated to one man, or to one body of men, it has invariably been grossly abused, and the sword of the people has been turned into a dagger against them. From the pressure of those evils, many nations have been induced expressly to forbid their governments the use of certain powers, without considering that the impotence of their supreme authority, would certainly be very prejudicial to them, and perhaps as fatal as the abuse of power. This experiment has repeatedly been made; it has frequently failed: and I believe that after several more experiments shall fully demonstrate the ill policies of this annihilating the powers of the nation, it will be clearly seen, that all the powers of the people ought to be delegated for their benefit, and that their true interest consists in the distribution of those powers in such a manner as shall, in its own operation, guard against the abuses which alone are dangerous to the people.

The Constitution of the United States appears to me to unite all the advantages both of the French and of the English, while it has avoided the evils of both. By that Constitution, the people have delegated the power of alteration, by vesting it in the Congress, together with the State Legislatures; while at the same time it has provided for alterations by the people themselves in their original character, whenever it shall evidently appear to be the wish of the people to make them. This article appears to be replete with wisdom; I believe it will stand the test of the severest examination, though according to the ideas emanating from Mr. Paine, and coming to us, at the same time, by reflection from the Secretary of State, it contains a very dangerous political heresy.

It is a maxim which I will not, I trust, be disputed, that no Government of which the people is not a constituent part, can secure their equal rights; but where this is the case, to cramp the operations of their own Government, with unnecessary restrictions, and forbid themselves to enact useful laws, what is it but to defeat the purposes of society, by the very act which gives it a permanent existence; to tie their own hands from an imaginary apprehension, that if left at liberty, they would administer poison to the body which nourishes them.

It is in the distribution of the national powers, it is in the independent spirit of the people, and not in the manuscript limitations of the legislative authority, that a nation is to secure the protection of its liberties. In this Commonwealth we have a Constitution, most parts of which are unalterable by our ordinary legislatures; it has existed but ten years, and already its operation has convinced us all, that several alterations in the system would be highly expedient. Our legislative body would be fully competent to the purpose, and, if they had the power, would readily make such alterations as might suit the convenience of the people; but they have no authority to act in these cases for the benefit of the people; and as the inconveniences to which this injudicious jealousy have subjected us, are not at this time of such importance, as to render the alterations of immediate or absolute necessity, we must wait our appointed time, and patiently submit to the operation of bad laws, because we have not chosen to invest our Legislature with the power of making good ones. Let us not be frightened, however, from the pursuit of our common interest by the words arbitrary power. Distribute the whole of your power in such a manner, as will necessarily prevent any one man, or body of men, or any possible combination of individual interests, from being arbitrary, but do not encumber your own representatives with shackles, prejudicial to your own interests; nor suffer yourselves, like the Spanish Monarch, of ridiculous memory, to be roasted to death, by denying to your servants the power of removing the fire from before you.

But although a Constitution, professedly unalterable by the common legislative authority, is of weight sufficient to prevent the enacting of many good laws, yet it will not always operate as a check upon your legislature. Such is the poverty of all human labors, that even a whole nation cannot express themselves upon paper with so much accuracy and precision, as not to admit of much latitude of explanation and construction. The legislature must always be allowed to judge of the intensions with which the instrument was formed, and to construe and explain accordingly the expressions which it contains. They sometimes think proper to violate the letter of the Constitution, by adhering to its spirit, and at other times they sacrifice the spirit, by adhering strictly to the letter. But when your Legislature undertakes to decide, that the spirit of the Constitution is directly contrary to its express letter, where is the power in the nation that should control them? The same power which will always be sufficient to control a Legislature, of which the people are a constituent part; it is the spirit of the people. Let your legislative and executive authorities be so constituted, as to prevent every essential or dangerous abuse of the powers delegated, but depend upon the honest and enlightened spirit of the people for security which you never will obtain, by merely withholding your powers, unless that spirit should be constantly kept up. Divide your power so that every part of it may at all times be used for your advantage, but in such a manner, that your rights may never depend upon the will of any one man or body of men; entrust even the power of altering your Constitution itself, because occasions may arise, when the use even of that power may be absolutely necessary for your own welfare, when, at the same time, it may be impossible for you to act in your original character, with the expedition necessary for your salvation; but reserve to yourselves a concurrent power of altering the Constitution in your own persons, because by the decay to which all the works of man are liable, it is possible that your Legislature may become incompetent to make such alterations as may be necessary. But when the people are constantly represented in the legislature, I believe they will never find it necessary to recur to their original character, in order to make any alterations which they may deem expedient, unless they deny the power of making them to their Legislature.

"But," says Mr. Paine, "there is a paradox in the idea of vitiated bodies reforming themselves." This must depend altogether upon the coincidence of the part vitiated, with the part which is to apply the remedy; for unless the defect itself necessary precludes the possibility of applying the power of reformation, the paradox ceases, and no more involves an absurdity, than that a physician should use his own prescriptions to cure himself of a disorder.

The very act by which septennial Parliaments were established in England, affords sufficient proof that the power of altering the Constitution itself ought to be delegated, and even exercised by the Government upon certain critical occasions. That act was made at a time when the kingdom was threatened with an immediate invasion, when a rebellion had but just been quelled, and when the peace and safety of the nation depended upon the use of this power by the Parliament; such was the opinion of the people at that time, and the act met with general approbation, from the general conviction of its necessity. Such occasions may happen in the history of every free people, and it is therefore proper that the power should be delegated. Upon the principles of equal liberty, upon the principles of public happiness, and therefore of political expedience, I think it may be fairly concluded, that Mr. Paine's preference of the French to the English Constitution, so far as it relates to this article, is not founded in truth.

LETTER VIII.

July 9, 1791

Sir, Mr. Paine has undertaken to compare the English and French Constitutions, upon the article of representation. He has of course admired the latter, and censured the former. This is unquestionably the most defective part of the English Constitution, but even the most essential of these defects appear to flow from the natural order of things, which a revolution in Government could not reform; from a state of society, when every principle of religion or of morality has lost its influence, and where the only shadow of virtue, public or private, remaining among a great majority of the people, is founded upon an imaginary point of honor, the relict of the exploded age of chivalry. Such at present is the situation of national character, both in England and in France. To attempt to govern a nation like this, under the form of a democracy, to pretend to establish over such beings a government which, according to Rousseau, is calculated only for a republic of Gods, and which requires the continual exercise of virtues beyond the reach of human infirmity, even in its best estate; it may possibly be among the dreams of Mr. Paine, but it is what even the National Assembly have not ventured to do; their system will avoid some of the defects, which the decays of time and the mutability of human affairs have introduced into that of the English, but I do not hesitate to affirm, that they have departed much further from the essential principles of popular representation, and that however their attachment to republican principles may have been celebrated, the *theory*, of their National Assembly is more remote from the spirit of democracy than the *practice* of the English House of Commons.

The grounds upon which Mr. Paine acknowledges his approbation of the French Constitution, are, that they have limited the number of their representatives, in proportion to the number of citizens who pay a tax of sixty sous *per annum*, and the duration of the Assembly to two years. It is certainly essential to the principles of representation, that there should be a frequent recurrence to the constituent body for election, because it is the only security of the constituent for the fidelity of the agent. It is the only practical responsibility by which the representative is bound. The term of seven years, for which the House of Commons is elected, weakens the responsibility too much, and is a proper object of constitutional reform; but by the French Constitution, there is no responsibility at all; no connection between the representative and his constituent; the *people* have not, even once in seven years, an opportunity to dismiss a servant who may have displeased them, or to re-elect another who may have given them satisfaction. There is, upon the French system, less dependence of the representative upon his constituent than in England, and the mode of election renders the biennial return of the choice almost wholly nugatory. It is not true that the French Constitution allows the privilege of voting for a representative in the National Assembly to every man who pays a tax of sixty sous *per annum.* Mr. Paine has mistaken the fact, for it is impossible that he should have intentionally misrepresented it, though it differs almost as much from his principles as from those of a real popular representation. It is as follows: every Frenchman, born or naturalized, of 25 years of age, who pays a tax equal to three days' labor, is not a hired servant, nor a bankrupt, nor the son of a deceased bankrupt (a very unjust qualification), shall be allowed to vote for — what? A representative to the National Assembly? By no means. Yet one would think the exclusions sufficiently severe, for a government founded upon equal rights of all men; but he shall vote for members of a certain Assembly; this Assembly is allowed to choose, not the representatives of the nation, but another body of electors, who are to be the immediate constituents of the Legislative Assembly. Thus, the supreme Legislative Council of the nation are to be the representatives of a representative body, whose constituents are the representatives of the people; and at every stage of this complicated representation, the free citizens of the state are excluded from their natural rights, by additional qualifications in point of property. Yet this is the system which we are told is to abolish aristocracy.

In the formation of the legislative body, the National Assembly contemplated three different objects of representation, the *persons* of the people, their *property,* and the *territory* which they inhabit. They have endeavored to establish a proportion compounded from the three; but in the refinement of their metaphysics and mathematics, they have lost the primary object itself, and the people are not represented.

But setting aside their calculations, what is the *essential* principle upon which the representation of the people in the Legislature is to be grounded? It is, that a freeman shall never be bound by any law, unless he has consented to it. It is impossible, except in a very small state, that every individual should personally give his voice, and therefore this practice of voting by representation was invented. In its most perfect state, it cannot fully answer the purpose of its institution, because every representative is actuated by several powerful motives, which could not operate upon his constituents. It is an *artificial democracy*, which never can perform completely the functions of the natural democracy; but imperfect as it always must be, no other contrivance has been hitherto devised, which could so effectually give their operation to the opinions of the people. In the theory of representation, it is a *personal* trust, by which a thousand individuals may authorize one man to express their sentiments upon every law which may be enacted for the benefit of the whole people: and therefore, in theory, every representative ought to be elected by the unanimous vote of his constituents; for how can a man be said to have been consulted in the formation of a law, when the agent authorized to express his opinion was not the man of his choice? Every pecuniary qualification imposed either on the electors, or as a condition of eligibility, is an additional restriction upon the natural democracy, and weakens the original purpose of the institution. Thus far the people of America have submitted to necessity in the constitution of their popular assemblies. But when the principle is abandoned so completely, that the individual citizen, even in the pretended exercise of his infinitesimal fragment of sovereignty, cannot possibly form an opinion, who will be the elector of the representative that is to be the depositary of his opinion in the acts of legislation. The assembly, thus formed, may indeed assume the name of a democracy; but it will no more be entitled to that appellation, than an ill-drawn miniature portrait to that of the animated original which it may profess to represent.

It is obvious that the reason why the National Assembly have chosen to refine their representation through so many strainers, was to avoid the violence, the tumults, the riots, which render almost all the populous towns in England a scene of war and blood at the period of Parliamentary elections. Time alone will inform us what the success of their system will be, even in this particular. Their elections, however, must be extremely expensive, and must open a thousand avenues to every sort of intrigue and venality. The National Assembly, as a body, will be in theory an aristocracy without responsibility. This aristocracy, thus constituted, are to possess the supreme power of the nation, limited only by a printed Constitution, subject to their own construction and explanation.

Happy, thrice happy the people of America! whose gentleness of manners, and habits of virtue, are still sufficient to reconcile the enjoyment of their natural rights with the peace and tranquility of their country; whose principles of religious liberty did not result from an indiscriminate contempt of all religion whatever, and whose equal representation, in their legislative councils, was founded upon an equality really existing among them, and not upon the metaphysical speculations of fanciful politicians, vainly contending against the unalterable course of events, and the established order of nature.

LETTER IX.

July 13, 1791

Sir, From the existence of game laws and of monopolies in England, Mr. Paine infers the wisdom of the National Assembly, who have decreed, that there shall be none in France. I shall not defend the game laws or the monopolies allowed in England; Mr. Paine's comparisons are made with the professed intention of showing the superiority of the French Constitution, and he has therefore always chosen his own ground of comparison. He might have pursued a system more consistent with truth and candor, but it would not have answered his purpose so effectually. The true drift of Mr. Paine's argument in this instance is this, *The English Parliament have enacted game laws that operate unequally. They have allowed more monopolies than are advantageous to the people; therefore the Legislature of a nation ought not to have the power to make any laws at all, relative either to game, or to monopolies.* This is Mr. Paine's principle, and it is the real ground upon which he prefers the French Constitution, not merely to that of England, but to those of every State in the American union. He infers that the English Constitution is bad, because under that Constitution certain bad laws have been enacted, and are not yet repealed. And he concludes that the French Constitution is excellent, because the universal freedom of the chase, and the universal freedom of trade are placed beyond the control of their Legislature. But the preservation of game is an object of public concern, and the Legislature of every country ought to have the power of making game laws for the benefit of the public. Whether the English Parliament have exerted unwisely this power which has been delegated to them or not, is a question altogether foreign to the purpose; we know that bad laws exist in every country under Heaven, but it is strange reasoning, to infer from thence, that there ought not to exist in the nation a power to make good ones. All the Legislatures in the United States have the power to enact game laws and to allow monopolies. They all of them exercise this power. We have game laws and monopolies in this Commonwealth, and yet no man complains that they are destructive to his liberty. If the French Constitution has placed the regulation of those objects beyond the reach of their ordinary legislative authority, they will soon find by their experiences of inconveniencies that the goodness of a Constitution does not depend upon the impotence of the Legislature.

In examining the next article, it is utterly impossible for me to do justice to the wit of Mr. Paine. The charge which he has so often repeated against Mr. Burke's book cannot be made against this production. You find here nothing of the "spouting rank of high-toned exclamation;" you do not even find the delicate sallies of elegant comedy. His own words must be quoted: "The French Constitution says, that to preserve the National representation from being corrupt, no member of the National Assembly shall be an officer of the government, a placeman or a pensioner. What will Mr. Burke place against this? I will whisper his answer: *Loaves and Fishes.*" And then he proceeds to show that the answer which he whispers for Mr. Burke is very ridiculous. There is, it must be acknowledged, something pleasant in this mode of managing an argument; but it is rather unfortunate that Mr. Paine should complain as an abuse of the English government, that it is "themselves accountable to themselves," so near to a passage which is most assuredly "himself undertaking to answer himself." Every person will acknowledge that the answer of *Loaves and Fishes* is very absurd; it is even too absurd for Mr. Burke in his original character; and the only circumstance that renders it perfectly accountable is, that it comes from Mr. Burke by his representative, who certainly never had from him any authority to misrepresent him so palpably.

Mr. Paine has seldom thought proper to answer even the few arguments contained in the book which is so obnoxious to him. Easy as it might have been to refute Mr. Burke's reasoning, he probably thought it easier to refute his own. He has hunted for epigrams where he ought to have sought arguments. In the pursuit of those epigrams he has been sometimes not unsuccessful in exposing the absurdity of his own reasoning, but a less passionate or more generous political polemic, would not have chosen to place his own inconsistencies to the account of his antagonist.

Mr. Paine has not, however, grounded his preference to the French Constitution upon truth, in this instance any more than in the other. The principle of excluding placemen, pensioners and executive officers from the national representation is acknowledged by the laws under the English Constitution as well as in that of France. The only possible advantage which the French can pretend to, is, that they have been more successful in its application. Mr. Paine might have said that it was not sufficiently extended by the English laws, and that it was by the French; and his opinion would have had its weight; but this would not answer his purpose; the French Constitution must at all events have a triumph; and a system so odious as the English Government, was not entitled to the benefits of common truth and justice. There are, however, several acts of Parliament; expressly excluding a great variety of placemen, pensioners and officers dependent upon the executive authority, from holding seats in the House of Commons. With respect to pensioners, their principle is more equitable than the total exclusion of the French. Every person holding a pension at the pleasure of the King, or for a term of years is excluded, because such a man may be too liable to be under the influence of the executive power; but if a man has received a pension for life, as a reward for services rendered his country, a pension which carries no dependence, and which can have no effect upon the legislative conduct of the person entitled to it, neither the English nor the Americans think that former services are a regular disqualification for the future; nor are they disposed to deprive any man of an invaluable privilege, merely because they have paid him for hazarding his life perhaps, or his fortune in their service.

But, says Mr. Paine, by the English Constitution "those who vote the supplies are the same persons who receive the supplies when voted, and are to account for the expenditure of those supplies to those who voted them; it is themselves accountable to themselves." This to be sure is very ingenious, but it is not in any sense true. The persons who vote the supplies are the House of Commons, the representatives of the nation. To them the King's ministers (and principally the Chancellor of the Exchequer) are accountable for the expenditure of the monies voted. The ministers may indeed be at the same time members of the House of Commons, and the system is perhaps defective in allowing a few individuals to be members of the body to whom they are accountable. It may be inconvenient, but is not at all absurd, and is purposely authorized by the English Constitution, because they consider the advantages as more than a balance for its inconveniences. The minister of the supreme executive office, states to the representatives of the nation, the sums necessary to defray the annual expenses of the kingdom. These representatives vote the assessment of such sums as they think necessary, and make the appropriations. The ministers then become accountable for the expenditures according to the previous appropriations, to that body of which they are indeed individual members, but of which they do not compose an hundredth part. Upon what principle then are we told that it is themselves accountable to themselves? They have indeed in France taken great pains to secure the independence of the legislative upon the executive authority; but they have not been equally cautious on the other side. Their executive is left totally at the mercy of the legislature, and must infallibly soon fall a sacrifice to their ambition.

The discussion of this subject would lead me far beyond my present intention. I have shown that the Constitution of England has adopted the principle of excluding citizens dependent upon the executive power, from the House of Commons; the French Constitution has done no more; and if they have carried the application of the principle further, that circumstance does not warrant the decided preference which Mr. Paine has so liberally bestowed; since it is only a difference of opinion upon the expediency of particular exclusions.

LETTER X.

July 20, 1791

Sir, The next article upon which Mr. Paine has pronounced the superiority of the French Constitution, is upon the subject of making war and peace. The right, he says, is placed where the expense is, that is, in the nation: whereas "in England, the right is said to reside in a *metaphor,* shown at the Tower for six pence of a shilling a piece." He answers himself again in this passage, and shows the folly of placing such a formidable right in a metaphor; but in this instance as in the former, there is much wit and no truth; and I must take the liberty to affirm in contradiction to Mr. Paine, that the French Constitution has not, nor could not place the right of declaring war, where the expense must fall; and that the English Constitution has not placed this right in a metaphor.

The expense of supporting wars must in all countries be defrayed by the nation, and every individual must bear his proportion of the burden. In free countries that proportion must always be determined by the representatives of the people; but the right of deciding when it may be expedient to engage in a war, cannot possibly be retained by the people of a populous and extensive territory, it must be a delegated power; and the French Constitution has vested it in the National Assembly. By the English

Constitution it is vested in the supreme executive officer; but to guard against the abuse of this formidable power, it has given to the representatives of the people, the exclusive right of providing for the support of the war, and of withholding the supplies, "the sinews of war," if it should ever be declared contrary to the sense of the people themselves. Mr. Paine supposes a perplexity, which is warranted neither by theory nor by the experience of history. "If the one rashly declares war," says he, "as a matter of right; and the other peremptorily withholds the supplies as a matter of right, the remedy becomes as bad or worse than the disease." But every war in England must be the war of the people: the King is in reality no more than the organ of the nation, and must be more than an idiot to declare a war, upon which he must depend altogether upon them for its support, without being certain of that support. Imaginary conclusions drawn by reasoning against the inevitable order of things, are unworthy of a politician, and should be left as a feeble resource for the satirist. To have given his objection even an appearance of plausibility, Mr. Paine should have mentioned an instance, when this clashing of the rights of the King and of the Commons has ever been productive of the ill effects which his fancy has sagaciously drawn from them.

Indeed Mr. Paine himself, upon further reflection, acknowledges the futility of his objection, and says "that in the manner the English nation is represented, it signifies not where this right resides, whether in the Crown or in the Parliament." But I apprehend, if the representation in England were as perfect as human wisdom could devise, their present system with respect to peace and war, would comprise all the advantages of the French system, and at the same time be free from many inconveniences, to which that must be liable.

It must be clear to everyone that the French have not, as Mr. Paine pretends, united the *right* and the *expense:* The impracticability of such a union, must be equally evident; and the only question which can establish a fair ground of comparison, between the two constitutions is, *Whether it is expedient to delegate to the legislative, or whether to the executive authority, the right of declaring war..*

As I am not yet a convert to Mr. Paine's opinion that a nation has a right to do what it pleases, I must be allowed to say that they have a right to make war upon their neighbors, without provocation. The people by their representatives must judge, when the provocation is sufficient to dissolve them from all the obligations of morality and humanity, by which nations are bound to preserve the blessings of peace. But when they have determined that the great law of self-preservation, to which all other laws must give way, or that the laws which they have enacted in consequence of the primitive contract which united all their power for the benefit of every individual, compel them to appeal for justice to the God of battles, then, the declaration of war, the formal act, by which they announce to the world their intention to employ the arm of power in their own defense, seems to be the proper attribute of the executive power. The difference, therefore, between the English and French constitutions, considered in this light, can involve only a question of propriety, and as such the English appears to me to deserve the preference.

If this idea should be considered as heretical, I must beg leave to call to my assistance the authority of Rousseau, a name still more respectable than that of Mr. Paine, because death has given the ultimate sanction to his reputation. "The act of declaring war," says he in his Social Compact, "and that of making peace, have been considered as acts of sovereignty, which is not the case; for either of those acts is not a law, but only an application of the law; a particular act which determines the operation of the law, as will be clearly perceived when the idea annexed to the word *law* shall be ascertained." The spirit of the English Constitution is perfectly agreeable to this idea.

But let us consider this subject a little further. Whenever a difference arises between two nations which may terminate in a war, it is proper and customary, that previous negotiations should be held, in order to use every possible means of settling amicably the dispute. These negotiations, the appointment of the agents by whom they are to be conducted, and the communication of the proposals for accommodation, which are respectively offered by either of the parties, are all appropriated to the executive department. When the restoration of peace becomes expedient in the opinion of the people, agents must again be appointed, and proposals of pacification must again be made. It is obvious to every man, that in the management of these concerns the utmost secrecy and despatch are frequently of essential necessity to the welfare of the people;

but what secrecy can ever be expected, when every instruction to an ambassador, every article of a proposed treaty, and every circumstance of information from the minister, in the progress of his operations, must be known to twelve hundred men assembled in the capital of the republic; what probability of despatch, when all these things must be debated in this Assembly of twelve hundred men; where everything must in the necessary order of events be opposed, by interested individuals and irritated factions, who may protract the discussion for months or years at their pleasure.

By the Constitution of the United States, it is true, the right of declaring war is vested in the Congress, that is, in the legislative power. But it is in the point of form that it agrees with the Constitution of France; it has wisely placed the management of all negotiations and treaties, and the appointment of all agents and ministers, in the executive department; and it has so thoroughly adopted in this instance the *principles* of the English Constitution, that although it has given the Congress the right of declaring war, which is merely a difference of form, it has vested in the President, with the advice of the Senate as his executive council, the right of making peace, which is implied in that of forming treaties. This is not the first instance in which Mr. Paine's principles attack those of the constitutions of his country. Highly as we may revere, however, the principles which we are under every obligation to support, we may without irreverence acknowledge that they partake of the human imperfection from which they originated, and if Mr. Paine's principles in opposition to them, are in any instance founded upon eternal truth, we may indulge the hope, that every necessary improvement will be adopted in a peaceable and amicable manner by the general consent of the people. But if the principles of Mr. Paine, or those of the French National Assembly, would lead us by a vain and delusive pretense of an impracticable union, between the right of declaring, and the expense of supporting a war, to the sacrifice of principles founded in immutable truth, if they could persuade us, by establishing in the legislative body all negotiations with foreign nations relative to war and peace, to open a thousand avenues for base intrigue, for furious faction, for foreign bribery, and domestic treason, let us remain immovably fixed at the banners of our constitutional freedom, and not desert the impregnable fortress of our liberties, for the unsubstantial fabric of visionary politicians.

LETTER XI.

July 27, 1791

Sir, The papers under the signature of Publicola have called forth a torrent of abuse, not upon their real author nor upon the sentiments they express, but upon a supposed author, and supposed sentiments.

With respect to the author, not one of the conjectures that have appeared in the public prints has been well grounded. The Vice-President[9] neither wrote nor corrected them; he did not give his sanction to an individual sentiment contained in them, nor did they "go to the press under the assumed patronage of his son."

With respect to the sentiments, to those who have read the pieces with attention, it is needless to say, that they are simply an examination of certain principles and arguments contained in a late pamphlet of Mr. Paine's, which are supposed to be directly opposite to principles acknowledged by the constitutions of our country. And the author challenges all the writers who have appeared in support of Mr. Paine's infallibility, to produce a single passage to these publications which has the most distant tendency to recommend either a monarchy or an aristocracy to the citizens of these States.

---

[9] The author's father, Vice-President John Adams

The writer never had the intention to defend the corruptions of the English Constitution; nor even its principles in theory, except such as were adopted in our own. Mr. Paine has drawn a comparison between certain parts of the English and French constitutions, in which are contained principles of government, that are not acknowledged by our own constitutions. So far as the principles of the English Constitution have been adopted by the Americans, I have defended them, and I am firmly convinced, that we cannot renounce them, without renouncing at the same time the happy governments with which we are favored. The question of superiority between the French and English constitutions, has no connection with a question relative to monarchy. If this be true, it must apply equally to the admirers of the French Constitution, and Mr. Paine himself is chargeable with having supported a monarchical institution. It is well known that by the French Constitution, a standing army of near 300,000 men is established, and placed beyond the annihilating arm of legislature. Is it possible that Mr. Paine should admire this Constitution, without being a friend to standing armies? The argument is the same, and the assertion might be made, with just as much truth, as that Publicola is an advocate for monarchy or for aristocracy.

When Mr. Paine says that a whole nation (by which it is admitted that he means a majority of the nation) have a right to do what it chooses, and when he says that before the formation of civil society every man has a natural right to judge in his own cause, it appears to me that he resolves all *right* into *power;* it is this opinion which I have combated, because it appears to me to be of the most pernicious tendency, and if it is not really contained in the pamphlet, I confess myself greatly mistaken. But the *enlightened* writers, who have defended the principles of Mr. Paine, differ so essentially in the ground they have taken, that the one or the other would certainly have been charged with propagating detestable heresies, had not the end sanctified the means, and the object of defending Mr. Paine, reconciled the inconsistency of their reasonings. One writer supports the principle through thick and thin; and tells you that the *will* of the contracting parties is the only circumstance that makes treaties obligatory. Another tells you that I have grossly misrepresented Mr. Paine, and that the national omnipotence which he establishes relates only to the internal concerns of the community. He agrees, however, that the will of the majority must be taken for the will of the whole nation, and that with respect to the formation of a government, a majority have a right to do what they please. So that it is no longer the "rights of men," but the rights of the majority which alone are unalienable.

Upon the question whether a constitution government can be made alterable otherwise than by the people in their original character, I have defended the constitutions of the United States against the principle of Mr. Paine, though in the re-publication of the paper in several of the southern papers, the passage which supports my opinion by the authority of the Constitution, is omitted.

Upon the article of representation, I have contended that the French representation is no representation of the people at all. Is there a man in the United States who would recommend it as a model to us? I have contended that our representation of the people is infinitely superior both to the French and the English; and this is said to be an abominable heresy.

Upon the subject of monopolies, of game laws, and of exclusions from the legislature, I have defended the *principles* adopted by our own constitutions, and not the abuses of the English Government. Upon that of war and peace I have done the same, and wherein Mr. Paine's observations have appeared to be founded upon any other foundation than truth, I have endeavored to show their fallacy. But a defense of monarchy or aristocracy was no more in my intention, than the defense of the Salic Law of descents was to that of Mr. Paine.

I shall now conclude these papers with requesting that those only who read them would judge upon their principles; and I am well persuaded, that the candor of the public will not take misrepresentation for reason, nor invective for argument.

Notes

Introduction
1. Joseph J. Ellis, *Passionate Sage* (W. W. Norton & Company, 1994), p. 29.
2. John Adams, *The Works of John Adams, Volume IV* (Little, Brown & Co., 1851), p. 587.
3. John Adams, *The Portable John Adams* (Penguin Books, 2004), p. 379.
4. John Adams, *The Portable John Adams* (Penguin Books, 2004), p. 360.
5. John Adams, *The Portable John Adams* (Penguin Books, 2004), p. 387.
6. Burke, Edmund, *Extract from the Speech of Edmund Burke, [9 February 1790]* (Founders Online, National Archives).
7. James Grant, *John Adams: Party of One* (Farrar, Straus and Giroux, 2005), p. 367; John Quincy Adams, *Writings of John Quincy Adams, Vol. 1 of 6* (Forgotten Books, 2012), p. 67.
8. James Grant, *John Adams: Party of One* (Farrar, Straus and Giroux, 2005), p. 370.

Bibliography

Adams, John. *The Portable John Adams.* New York: Penguin Books, 2004.

Adams, John. *The Works of John Adams, Volume IV.* Boston: Little, Brown & Co., 1851.

Adams, John Quincy. *Writings of John Quincy Adams: Vol. 1 of 6.* Forgotten Books, 2012; Adams, John Quincy. *Writings of John Quincy Adams: Vol. I.* New York: The MacMillan Company, 1913.

Ellis, Joseph. *Passionate Sage: The Character and Legacy of John Adams.* New York: W.W. Norton & Company, 1993.

Grant, James. *John Adams: Party of One.* New York: Farrar, Straus and Giroux, 2005.

McCullough, David. *John Adams.* New York: Simon & Schuster, 2001.

Norman, Jesse. *Edmund Burke: The First Conservative.* New York: Basic Books, 2013.

Publicola. *Observations on Paine's Rights of man, in a series of letters, Third edition.* Edinburgh: J Dickson, J and J Fairbairn; ECCO Print Editions.

www.ingramcontent.com/pod-product-compliance
Lightning Source LLC
Chambersburg PA
CBHW031428290426
44110CB00011B/569